PACIFIC ELECTRIC RAILWAY

Opposite: The morning of June 19, 1955, was gloomy, not because fog had rolled in from the coast, but because the end of an era was taking place. A handful of rail fans and former passengers gathered to see the final Pacific Electric (PE) subway car pass from the mouth of Belmont Tunnel into what the banner draped on her front summed up so well: "To . . . Oblivion." (Historical photograph by Donald Duke; courtesy of the Donald Duke collection.)

PACIFIC ELECTRIC RAILWAY

Steve Crise, Michael A. Patris,
and the Pacific Electric Railway
Historical Society

To Donald Duke—photographer, author, publisher, philanthropist, and friend.

Copyright © 2011 by Steve Crise, Michael A. Patris, and the Pacific Electric Railway Historical Society
ISBN 978-0-7385-7586-5

Library of Congress Control Number: 2011923774

Published by Arcadia Publishing
Charleston, South Carolina

Printed in the United States of America

For all general information, please contact Arcadia Publishing:
Telephone 843-853-2070
Fax 843-853-0044
E-mail sales@arcadiapublishing.com
For customer service and orders:
Toll-Free 1-888-313-2665

Visit us on the Internet at www.arcadiapublishing.com

On the Front Cover: After leaving Redondo Beach and heading inbound (north) to Los Angeles, interurban car 841 headed toward Playa del Rey in this late 1930s photograph. This section of right-of-way, closed in 1941, is part of the Strand bike path, which stretches between Torrance Beach (south) and Will Rogers State Beach (north). The modern image was taken near the intersection of Vista Del Mar and Waterview Streets. (Historical photograph by Charles D. Savage; courtesy of the Donald Duke collection.)

On the Back Cover: The Pacific Electric Railway building was the backdrop for this pair of images shot in downtown Los Angeles at Sixth and Main Streets. Car 1051 started out on the Pasadena Short Line, headed west on Sixth Street, then turned right on Main Street and headed north in this c.1940s image. The PE building has recently completed a renovation to residential lofts. (Historical photograph courtesy of the Jack Finn collection.)

Contents

Acknowledgments		vii
Introduction		ix
1.	Western District	11
2.	Southern District	39
3.	Eastern District	61
4.	Northern District	75

Acknowledgments

Many thanks go out to those who have helped inspire and create this work. Most of all, our deepest gratitude goes to the late Jack Finn, founder of the Pacific Electric Railway Historical Society (www.peryhs.org). Jack's accumulation of images and the eventual donation of that archive to the Mount Lowe Preservation Society, Inc. provided the basis for this book. In addition, sincere thanks to longtime friend and rail enthusiast Alan Weeks, whose insights, recollections, gentle prodding, and encouragement keep us on track toward the ultimate goal of having the largest online archive of images from the Pacific Electric and Los Angeles Railways available to as many people as possible.

Others who have been inspirational and helpful with the completion of this project include Don Baker, Matthew Barrett of the Metropolitan Transit Authority (MTA), Joe Bonino, Jim Bunte, Bill Everett, Tom Gray, Mike Jarel, Bobby McDearmon, Mike McGinley, Jeffrey Moreau, Charles Seims, John Smatlak, Gary Starre, Elbert Swerdfeger, Jim Walker of the MTA, Matt Wiles, and Chuck Wilson. Very special thanks go to fellow rail fan and collector Craig Rasmussen, who has provided information and numerous images not only to this book, but also to our ongoing project of digitizing over 5,000 images of the Pacific Electric Railway, which can be seen at www.peryhs.org.

Institutions that have provided assistance include Historic Aerials (www.historicaerials.com); Covina Valley Historical Society; Jen Johnson of the Book Shop in Monrovia, California; Orange Empire Railway Museum (OERM); Pacific Railroad Society (PRS); and the Mount Lowe Preservation Society, Inc. (www.mountlowe.org).

Invaluable contributors who are no longer with us include our dear friend and revered railroad photographer Donald Norman Duke, whose work inspired a very young Steve Crise to begin photographing railroads decades ago; Ralph Melching; Ernie Leo; Charles D. Savage; Harold Stewart; Ira Swett (and his Interurban Special publications); Chard Walker; Bill "Marvin" Whyte; and Ray Younghans. Finally, those who provide special inspiration on an ongoing basis are Yoko Mazza and Mudd Patris, for their eternal patience and tolerance, and Cay Sehnert, a true friend and editor extraordinaire.

All historical images used in this book are from the Pacific Electric Railway Historical Society archives, now housed with the Mount Lowe Preservation Society, Inc., unless otherwise credited. All current images are courtesy of the co-author, photographer Steve Crise (www.scrise.com).

Introduction

The Pacific Electric Railway and its 1,100 miles of track connecting Southern California's many diverse communities with each other have had numerous volumes dedicated to photography, the railway's history, and even rumored conspiracy theories regarding its demise. But this work is different because the Pacific Electric Railway Historical Society, now part of the nonprofit Mount Lowe Preservation Society, Inc., has been fortunate enough to work from an incredible collection of material donated by the late Jack Finn.

As an avocation, Jack began accumulating local rail images when he was a teenager growing up near the local Glendale Line of the Pacific Electric Railway in the 1950s. He would later go on to perform slide shows and publish a newsletter for traction enthusiasts; he eventually founded the Pacific Electric Railway Historical Society in 1999. Almost immediately, Jack began printing monographs built on stories from individuals who had valuable memories, specialized knowledge, or specific links to the Pacific Electric.

When Jack died in 2006, he had not yet fulfilled his dream of sharing all his photographs and information with the public, so he bequeathed his material to the Mount Lowe Preservation Society, Inc. Since then, nearly all of the more than 5,000 images have been scanned and are in the process of being cleaned up, catalogued, and added to the society's website, www.peryhs.org. The interactive database on the site allows visitors to add comments and information, which is then permanently linked to the image. For instance, if a visitor to the site happens to know an individual, the year, or location in a photograph, it can be added for all to share. Expanding on that concept, photographer Steve Crise's modern images from this book can be located on a map and viewed on the website, so as to ascertain the exact locations where historical parts of the railway once existed. This will give readers the opportunity to go and see for themselves where local history actually took place.

Steve has also wanted to do a book on the Pacific Electric Railway since his youth, but it was our mutual friendship with renowned railroad photographer Donald Duke that really set all this into realistic motion. Sadly, "Duke" has passed away as well, but not before we were able to share in his great archive of images and photography. Some of that material is also shared in this book.

The four districts of the Pacific Electric Railway—Western, Southern, Eastern, and Northern—represent a vast area of land in four counties: Los Angeles, Orange, San Bernardino, and Riverside. Before 1900, there were many independent railroad and horse-car lines that were bought up by Henry Huntington and then incorporated into what became known as the Pacific Electric Railway in 1901.

Ten years later in 1911, the Southern Pacific Railroad purchased most of the stock in the Pacific Electric Railway, which included nearly every railroad interest Huntington owned, except for the Los Angeles, or LA Railway, also known as the LARy, or the Yellow Cars. This Great Merger of 1911 is mentioned in some of the captions to acknowledge that there did previously exist routes that were not initiated by Huntington himself. Not all of those bought-out entities are identified, as they were numerous and there is not enough space in this visual history to make all the necessary acknowledgements.

The Railroad Boosters are mentioned in this book and, in particular, Ralph Melching. Ralph passed away several years ago, but left an amazing body of work with his photography, some of which may be seen here. Donald Duke and Ralph Melching were friends for decades, and we all got to know one another by telling stories and sharing photographs of "the good old days." Ralph and his brother Wayne (who predeceased Ralph by many years) were two of the six individuals who began the Railroad Boosters back in 1936 when much of the equipment and lines covered in this book were still operational.

Among the places the Railroad Boosters traveled to were the Pacific Electric Railway's Torrance Shops, where cars were built and maintained, several regions throughout Southern California along PE lines, and the one most everyone talks about, the Mount Lowe Railway. Since there is a Mount Lowe Railway book that is also a part of Arcadia's Then and Now series nearing completion, we have purposely not included any Mount Lowe images in this volume. It was challenging enough to edit down to the images here, and there is certainly ample material for a second or third volume of this nature.

The Railroad Boosters grew as an organization, and by 1949, they had changed their name to the Pacific Railroad Society, or as it is affectionately know by many, PRS. PRS incorporated in 1957 and became a nonprofit entity by 1980. Since then, they have occupied the former Atchison, Topeka & Santa Fe Railroad Depot in San Dimas, where they operate the Pacific Railroad Museum, which is open to the public and staffed by PRS volunteers. The PRS is thanked and acknowledged not only for their help in maintaining Ralph Melching's and other photographic collections, but for their ongoing support of researchers and rail fans who visit their facility.

John Smatlak and the Orange Empire Railway Museum (OERM) have been consistently helpful with their maps, photographs, and knowledge of the Pacific Electric Railway, not to mention the wonderful preservation work they have been doing for more than half a century on rare and obsolete railroad rolling stock. For the opportunity to see some Pacific Electric Railway trolleys in action, going there is as good as it gets.

The possible, yet unrealized, retention and modernization of the Pacific Electric Railway's infrastructure stands in Southern California's public transportation history as a stunning case of missed opportunity. But even this does not diminish the remarkable level of service reached over the evolution of such a comprehensive system, serving such scattered geographies and demographics. Both those who made this achievement possible and those who seek to honor it by keeping its story alive may look upon their endeavors with pride.

CHAPTER 1

WESTERN DISTRICT

A trip from downtown Los Angeles to Santa Monica covered 20 miles in just over an hour, which was a popular and inexpensive way to get out on the weekends. Car 107, built by the St. Louis Car Company about 1930, pauses during a fan trip. This c. 1950 image shows the Pacific Electric (PE) Station and Trolley Cafe on Ocean Avenue. (Historical photograph by Donald Duke; courtesy of the Donald Duke collection.)

Business car 1299 pauses in front of USC's Mudd Hall around 1950. Once part of the old Airline, this right-of-way is under construction for the current Expo Line, as it runs down Exposition Boulevard. Eventually, the Metropolitan Transit Authority (MTA) hopes to build this line to Santa Monica. Note the time on the clock; photographer Steve Crise took the modern image at exactly the same time as the historical image. (Historical photograph by Donald Duke; courtesy of the Donald Duke collection.)

An electric switch engine heads west along Exposition Boulevard between Chesapeake and Farmdale Avenues, where Dorsey High School is located. Westinghouse made most of these engines, but the Pacific Electric later made their own copies, nicknaming them "Juice Jacks." This freight consist was shot in the early 1950s. At the time of this writing, cars are being tested for the MTA's soon-to-open Expo Line. (Historical photograph by Donald Duke; courtesy of the Donald Duke collection.)

The Los Angeles and Independence Railroad first carried freight on this former narrow gauge steam line in 1875. In 1877, the Southern Pacific (SP) purchased it for service to its Santa Monica wharf. PE took over in 1911 and provided passenger service through 1953, with SP's continued freight use until 1989. Bordered by Northvale Road in Cheviot Hills, it's currently being considered for part of the Expo Line expansion to Santa Monica. (Historical photograph by Donald Duke; courtesy of the Donald Duke collection.)

Pacific Electric Railway employee and rail fan Walter Abbenseth caught car 5111 squeezing by the Parkhurst Building on this July 26, 1952, fan trip. The private right-of-way, located near the northwest corner of Pier and Main Streets, is now open only to foot traffic. The Parkhurst Building survives on the National Register of Historic Places; car no. 5111, built in 1922 by the St. Louis Car Company, was not so lucky. (Historical photograph courtesy of the Jack Finn collection.)

A three-car train led by car 973 heads out from Hill Street to Venice Boulevard on the Venice Short Line in 1940. Three flagmen are posted on the cars as the turn is made. In the modern image, photographer Steve Crise catches a compressed natural gas (CNG) Metro Rapid bus in the same spot decades later. (Historical photograph by and courtesy of Tom Gray.)

Vineyard Junction split traffic between Beverly Hills to the northwest and the Venice Short Line to the west. While Venice Beach traffic was good, World War I put an end to any consideration of a possible Vineyard Subway. Looking northwest from the West Boulevard bridge decades later, a Metro bus approaches Vineyard Junction, heading toward Venice Beach. (Historical photograph by Ralph Melching; courtesy of the PRS collection.)

On February 9, 1941, a two-car train is seen inbound via the Venice Short Line at the La Cienega viaduct. The PCC (Presidents' Conference Committee) cars pictured here only ran a short time on this line due to the rough track, which was a contributing factor to the line closing by September 1950. The modern image shows articulated CNG Rapid Line bus 9296, manufactured by North American Bus Industries. (Historical photograph by Ralph Melching; courtesy of the PRS collection.)

On March 25, 1942, the Los Angeles Times reported, "Two Army Men Die of Injuries Following Three-Way Collision," which took place at Venice and Lincoln Boulevards in Venice. Eight soldiers and twelve civilians were also injured when a PE Limited, an Army truck, and a private automobile collided. The commercial building at the extreme right still stands. However, the Shell station in the historical image was torn down just before the current image was taken. (Historical photograph courtesy of the Jack Finn collection.)

Western District

Looking east on Culver Boulevard at Duquesne, car 5111 heads toward downtown Los Angeles on July 26, 1953. A tree-lined median has replaced the Pacific Electric Railway tracks, but down another block east at Washington Boulevard, the Culver Hotel still stands. Culver Junction was 9.25 miles from PE's building at the corner of Sixth and Main Streets. (Historical photograph courtesy of the Jack Finn collection.)

Photographer Ralph Melching wrote about this image: "Birney car 336, last day of service on Lagoon Line at Playa del Rey, 7-12-36, 1:40 p.m." The Lagoon Line ran from a private right-of-way between Pacific and Ocean Avenues. The Moorish-style building at 200 Culver Boulevard and Montreal Street (at left) is still standing. Neoplan CNG Metro Local bus 6311 is heading toward downtown Los Angeles. (Historical photograph by Ralph Melching; courtesy of the PRS collection.)

Not much from the past remains today at the intersection of Culver Boulevard and Vista del Mar in Playa del Rey, except for the historic two-story structure on the left at 179 Culver Boulevard. The earlier photograph was shot on December 24, 1939, but the current image shows that Metro busses still service this route. (Historical photograph by Ralph Melching; courtesy of the PRS collection.)

In this early 1950s photograph, car 728 heads toward downtown Los Angeles along Sunset Boulevard at Douglas Street in Echo Park. The Hollywood Line, of which this was part, originally ran from the Subway Terminal Building at Fourth and Hill Streets and was Los Angeles's first subway, opening in November 1926. The last car run on the Subway-Hollywood Line left Beverly Hills on September 26, 1954. (Historical photograph courtesy of the Tom Gray collection.)

Car 106, built by the St. Louis Car Company, heads along Echo Park Avenue at Cerro Gordo Street, on May 27, 1950, just about four months before the line was closed down. The Elysian Park Railway Company originally built local service to Echo Park via the Echo Park Avenue Line as a horse car line in 1899. (Historical photograph by Ralph Melching; courtesy of the PRS collection.)

Photographer Steve Crise shot this modern photograph on Labor Day, September 6, 2010, fifty-six years to the day after the historical image that was captured by an unknown photographer, just east of the corner of Hollywood Boulevard and Vine Street. A Metro bus keeps up the route the former PCC car 5024 did, heading toward downtown Los Angeles. Many of the original historic buildings still stand along this route. (Historical photograph courtesy of the Jack Finn collection.)

The historic architecture is about all that remains at the intersection of Holloway Drive, Croft Avenue, and Santa Monica Boulevard. Not only is Bekins Moving and Storage gone, so is the Pacific Electric Railway, which once skirted this well-known landmark. Car 5096 is passing Hacienda Park, a stop along this route. (Historical photograph courtesy of the Jack Finn collection.)

Looking east past the Beverly Hills Post Office, a PE caboose is heading inbound toward West Hollywood. The construction seen at the time of this modern image is the site of the Annenberg Performing Arts Center, where the former post office building is to become the foyer of the new entertainment plaza. This line closed in 1971. (Historical photograph by Donald Duke; courtesy of the Donald Duke collection.)

Western District

Washington's birthday, February 22, 1953, was when this fan trip took place along Santa Monica Boulevard at Beverly Glen. Car 5028 is stopped for a photo op on the steel bridge, which was removed from Fletcher Drive in Glendale and repurposed here. Removal of the bridge from its second home took place in 1986, making it hard to believe there were ever tracks along this street. (Historical photograph by Donald Duke; courtesy of the Donald Duke collection.)

In Atwater, the only remains from the days of the PE are the tapered concrete bridge footings, which are possibly going to be saved as part of an open green space or historical park. Currie's Ice Cream is long gone, but the gas stations at Fletcher and Riverside Drives linger; Chevron remains unchanged and Richfield has become Arco. (Historical photograph by Donald Duke; courtesy of the Donald Duke collection.)

WESTERN DISTRICT

A PCC car in regular service heads in toward downtown Los Angeles and the Subway Terminal Building at Fourth and Hill Streets as it nears the overpass of Sunset Boulevard, from which both images were taken. The modern image shows a Line 92 Metro bus heading to Main Street and Olympic Boulevard, in nearly the same position as the PCC car in the earlier image. (Historical photograph courtesy of the Jack Finn collection.)

Car 5106 has just passed under the Sunset Boulevard Bridge as it travels outbound along Glendale Boulevard in nearly the same spot as the car in the previous historical image. The trolley is heading to Glendale, and the Metro bus in the modern image is heading to Sylmar. In the background of the vintage photograph, the dome of Aimee Semple McPherson's Angeles Temple is visible just beyond the bridge. (Historical photograph courtesy of the Jack Finn collection.)

In Glendale, the Verdugo Mountains topping Brand Boulevard and the 100-foot Art Deco column at the Alex Theater are two landmarks that have withstood time. The PE closed down the Glendale Line on June 19, 1955, and almost immediately, local businesses felt the loss of revenue. Woolworth's once stood at Wilson Avenue on the left, and now only the name in the terrazzo remains. The modern bus is heading to Los Angeles. (Historical photograph courtesy of the Jack Finn collection.)

Car 5007 swings south on Brand Boulevard from Glenoaks in this pre-1955 image. Looking north, the Catholic Church of the Incarnation (church, school, and community center) on the left at 1001 N. Brand Boulevard is still serving the community. Just a few blocks north is Mountain Avenue, terminus of the PE line. Two modern buses currently serve the area—the first one from the MTA and the second a Glendale Bee Line local. (Historical photograph courtesy of the Jack Finn collection.)

WESTERN DISTRICT

Car 5019 makes its way along Glenoaks Boulevard at Olive Avenue, pacing a 1949 Ford woody station wagon and 1950 Studebaker. The Chevron gas station appears to be the only thing withstanding the test of time. Five blocks north at Cypress Street, this single-track line reached its terminus. Note that the Metro bus in the modern image is in nearly the same spot the trolley once occupied. (Historical photograph courtesy of the Jack Finn collection.)

The North Hollywood PE/SP Station still stands near the corner of Lankershim and Chandler Boulevards, waiting to be restored. In the historical image, car 5132 (left) is heading to the Subway Terminal Building and car 5150 (right) is bound for Van Nuys. The articulated bus in the modern image is at the eastern terminus of the Metro Orange Line and the Northern terminus of the Metro Red Line (Historical photograph by Donald Duke; courtesy of the Donald Duke collection.)

Car 5164 heads out from the Subway Terminal tunnel in this early 1950s photograph just before operations stopped in June 1955. For many years, the tunnel remained unsecured until construction of the neighboring Belmont Station Apartments prompted its closure. Artist Tait Roelofs painted a life-size, glow-in-the-dark mural of a Red Car on the tunnel face, which adjoins a dog run. (Historical photograph by Donald Duke; courtesy of the Donald Duke collection.)

This late afternoon shot of Toluca Yard was taken in 1942. Car 5002 is heading inbound and car 659 is heading out from the Subway Terminal Tunnel. Today, the odd shaped piece of property, bordered by Lucas Avenue and Glendale Boulevard, is home to the Belmont Station Apartments. Behind this structure is where the dog run and mural of the Red Car coming out of the sealed tunnel can be found. (Historical photograph by Ralph Melching; courtesy of the Donald Duke collection.)

WESTERN DISTRICT

The Cahuenga Pass is the location for this rare photographic moment, as PCC car 5011 passes the Mulholland Car Stop in the center of the Hollywood Freeway, on its way to downtown Los Angeles. This fan trip was special, because PCC cars did not usually travel this line. In the modern photograph, a Metro bus heads northbound into the San Fernando Valley on Cahuenga Boulevard East. (Historical photograph by Donald Duke; courtesy of the Donald Duke collection.)

CHAPTER

SOUTHERN DISTRICT

In 1910, Charles Lawrence, official photographer for the Pacific Electric Railway, created this image of the four tracks looking north from the signal bridge at Slauson Junction. The east-west tracks belong to the Santa Fe Railway's Redondo Beach Branch Line and the tracks heading southeast (to the bottom right) are Pacific Electric's Whittier-Fullerton-Yorba Linda Line. The Southern District included all lines in Orange County and the southeastern part of Los Angeles County. (Historical photograph by Charles Lawrence; courtesy of the Donald Duke collection.)

Heading south, Los Angeles Railway's car 662 travels on the F-Line, and PE car 628 motors along from Watts at the intersection of Spring Street (at left), Main Street (at right) and Ninth Street. Looking north at the right, the Hotel Cecil still survives today. It is hard to believe there are more billboards and advertisements in the historical photograph. The Watts Local car terminated at Sixth and Main Streets. (Historical photograph by H.L. "Harvey" Kelso; courtesy of the Michael Patris collection.)

SOUTHERN DISTRICT

The intersection of Ninth and San Pedro Streets looks like well-orchestrated chaos as the LA Transit Line steel double truck Type "H" car 1236 and PE's 4637 Blimp maneuver around two vintage automobiles. In the modern fashion district image, photographer Steve Crise used a 12-foot ladder to capture the two busses mimicking the two trolleys from the earlier image. Note the building on the northwest corner that still survives today. (Historical photograph courtesy of the Jack Finn collection.)

SOUTHERN DISTRICT

Looking north, PE car 1537 clears the construction along the 10 Freeway at Long Beach Boulevard in 1961. Shown to the left in the modern photograph, the vintage tracks and switch can be seen poking through the decomposing asphalt. The chain-link fence area under the freeway appears to be private storage. The white truck is parked at 16th Street. (Historical photograph courtesy of the Jack Finn collection.)

The American Olive Company was the namesake for Amoco Junction, shown in this c. 1953 photograph. Amoco Tower was built on the steel signal bridge above the tracks. PE car 1812 might have been on a fan trip when this vintage image was captured with a Rollei 2 1/4" camera. In the modern image, the Metro Blue Line is heading south during rush hour in a three-car configuration. (Historical photograph by Bill Whyte; courtesy of the Steve Crise collection.)

Looking south, things have changed quite a bit at the intersection of Slauson Boulevard at the four tracks since the days when PE's Long Beach Limited car headed into Los Angeles. The Santa Fe tracks appear in the foreground, with Slauson Station and Tower on the extreme right. The modern image shows a Metro Blue Line train heading south on elevated tracks at rush hour. (Historical photograph by Bill Whyte; courtesy of the Steve Crise collection.)

In 1952, an unknown photographer shot this three-car Los Angeles Limited train heading north out of Long Beach along Long Beach Blvd at Eighth Street. Car 428, called a "Blimp" by the Pacific Electric, was brought to Southern California from the Oregon Electric Railway. The modern image also depicts a three-car train from the Blue Line heading south toward the still-standing Long Beach Post Office Building. (Historical photograph courtesy of the Jack Finn collection.)

On Sunday, January 11, 1959, at 3:30 p.m., Mrs. Ransdell steered her blue 1955 Ford Club Sedan southbound on American Avenue (now Long Beach Boulevard) at 16th Street, intending to turn left in front of PE 1537, but her car died on the tracks. The resulting collision pushed the Ford approximately 115 feet north, but did not injure the driver. A special thanks goes to Gary Starre for this fascinating information. (Historical photograph by Bill Whyte; courtesy of the Steve Crise collection.)

Just passing the Watts Towers along the Bellflower Line, car 435 heads toward downtown Los Angeles. The black letter "S" on the white square painted on the telephone pole denotes a slow zone. This line, originally opened by the Los Angeles Interurban Railway Company in 1905, was known early on as the Santa Ana Line for the Pacific Electric. Passenger service was cut back in 1950 and finally abandoned in 1958. (Historical photograph courtesy of the Jack Finn collection.)

SOUTHERN DISTRICT

Heading northbound, Blimp 311 pauses in front of the Bellflower Station with Bellflower Boulevard in the foreground. This station has been restored to an earlier iteration than this vintage photograph depicts, where it sports columns and a Railway Express Agency sign. This right-of-way is currently used as a walkway and bike path. The West Santa Ana Transit Corridor (current name) wants to eventually link Paramount and Santa Ana. (Historical photograph courtesy of the Jack Finn collection.)

PE's 1218 leads a two-car train south, passing the Santa Ana River trestle on April 7, 1945, just six years before these cars would be scrapped by Kaiser Steel. The current image was taken on the northeastern edge of the Willowick Municipal Golf Course. A special thanks goes to Mike McGinley for pointing out that this image, commonly mistaken as the San Gabriel River, is actually the Santa Ana River. (Historical photograph by Charles D. Savage; courtesy of the Donald Duke collection.)

For the PRS fan trip on May 13, 1951, car 5061 is heading eastbound on Fourth Street after crossing Main Street. The vintage Otis Building in the middle of the modern photograph is barely perceptible in the earlier image, just above the roof of the streetcar. Kress and Company is no longer in business. These pictures were taken at the corner of Fourth and Bush Streets. (Historical photograph courtesy of the Jack Finn collection.)

Surviving Railroad Boosters remember their third trip to Fullerton on Sunday, May 2, 1937, called "Off the Beaten Track," because they stopped car 1261 on the old bridge and scrambled down the hill to shoot this image. Passenger service only lasted another year, but freight service continued for quite some time. In the modern image, the Orange County Transit Authority's articulated bus heads for Costa Mesa, turning right from Berkeley Avenue onto Harbor Boulevard. (Historical photograph by Ralph Melching; courtesy of the PRS collection.)

SOUTHERN DISTRICT

Another Railroad Boosters fan trip that headed south was the 18th one, taken on May 18, 1939, also called "Off the Beaten Track." Car 1205 is shown beside the Pacific Electric/Southern Pacific Station at 136 E. Commonwealth Avenue in Fullerton. It's fortunate that the station has remained intact, but the Spadra Ristorante was not so lucky, having gone out of business as of this writing. (Historical photograph by Ralph Melching; courtesy of the PRS collection.)

On a September 16, 1956, fan trip, car 5121 overtakes a new Volkswagen in Wilmington along B Street, now known as Harry Bridges Boulevard. Not only has the street name changed in the modern image, the whole area appears to be undergoing a major transformation and rehabilitation known as the Harry Bridges Boulevard Buffer Project, which proposes a large green belt between residential and commercial properties. (Historical photograph courtesy of the Jack Finn collection.)

PE car 379 has made its way to the end of the line in San Pedro at the intersection of Bandini and Santa Cruz Streets, looking north. The wooden apartment building on the right corner, just beyond the intersection, has survived all these years, as have many palm trees. The little market on the right side of the historical image has been torn down and a parking lot has taken its place. (Historical photograph by Ralph Melching; courtesy of the PRS collection.)

The significant story about wooden car 1001 is that it still survives today, living at Orange Empire Railway Museum (OERM), in Perris, California. Pacific Electric Railway employee Walter Abbenseth purchased this 1913 model car in 1954 for several hundred dollars after it had been declared surplus. Photographer Steve Crise immortalized Abbenseth, now deceased, with his car in 2003; the earlier image was captured in 1946. (Historical photograph by Ray Younghans; courtesy of the Craig Rasmussen collection.)

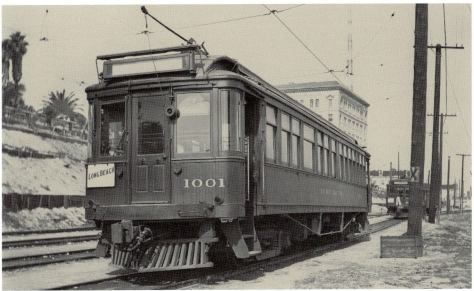

SOUTHERN DISTRICT

PCC cars in El Segundo were an uncommon sight, but not for those on this fan trip on February 22, 1956. This 5000-class car stopped for a photo op in front of the El Segundo PE/SP Station. The El Segundo Line closed for passenger service in 1930 and only serviced freight after that for many years. The station was on Grand Avenue at Eucalyptus Drive, looking northeast. (Historical photograph by Charles D. Savage; courtesy of the Donald Duke collection.)

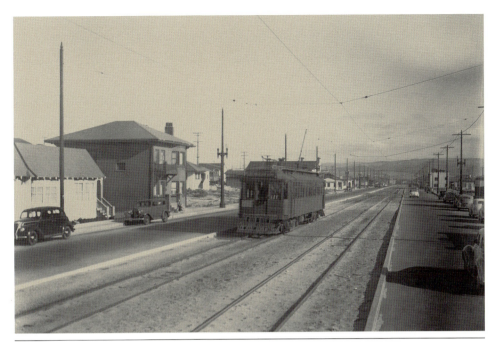

Railroader Mike Jarel recommended this uncommon 1940 image of a 900-class car, looking south along the 700 block of Hermosa Avenue toward Palos Verdes. The two wooden apartment buildings on the left have survived, and the former right-of-way has become a concrete median with middle of the street parking. (Historical photograph by Frank Bradford; courtesy of the Craig Rasmussen collection.)

SOUTHERN DISTRICT

The PE's old concrete viaduct still stands over Torrance Boulevard from the days when it serviced the Columbia Steel Mill, northwest of this intersection. An early 1950s fan trip caught car 5128 making its way west, past some freight cars sitting on a siding. Beyond the bridge lies Western Avenue. Passenger service ended on this line by January 1940, but Union Pacific Freight still operates today. (Historical photograph by Donald Duke; courtesy of the Donald Duke collection.)

Newport Beach Limited boxmotor 1647 heads inbound along Electric Avenue to Los Angeles with a Pacific Electric bus stopped at the tracks behind it at Main Street around 1938, two years before closure to passenger traffic. Looking southeast, a modern bus visits where the historical bus once sat, adjacent to the grass median along Electric Avenue where the original right-of-way once ran. (Historical photograph by Charles D. Savage; courtesy of the Jack Finn collection.)

SOUTHERN DISTRICT

Unfortunately, the date and photographer's name for this shot of a Newport-Balboa Limited car in Balboa are unknown. What is known, however, is that the old buildings on the right side of the image have survived, long past the line closure date of June 30, 1950. The Newport Balboa Line was 39.66 miles from Los Angeles, the farthest south one could travel in the Southern District. (Historical photograph courtesy of the Jack Finn collection.)

CHAPTER 3

EASTERN DISTRICT

The Eastern District of the Pacific Electric Railway included lines in Riverside and San Bernardino Counties, but in this book, some areas east of downtown Los Angeles that were actually in the Northern District are included.

Looking north up Mountain View Avenue at the Santa Fe crossing, car 101 heads south along the Colton Local Line in 1937 near Arrowhead Station. (Historical photograph courtesy Craig Rasmussen collection.)

This historical view of the Pacific Electric Station and building at Sixth and Main Streets, taken on December 21, 1935, shows a two-car train heading outbound for Pomona. This is the eastern elevation of the building that originally boasted more than 500 offices and has only recently been converted to high-end residential lofts, starting at $1,300 per month for a studio and $2,800 per month for two bedrooms. (Historical photograph by Ralph Melching; courtesy of the PRS collection.)

Since 1946, New Avenue in San Gabriel has undergone some major changes. What was once Pacific Electric Railway double track heading east from Los Angeles through a mostly rural San Gabriel Valley, Interstate 10 has evolved into one of the busiest freeways in Southern California. Santa Fe steam locomotive 3751 is out on a rare run, heading back to Los Angeles from San Bernardino as it travels over the New Avenue underpass. (Historical photograph courtesy of the Jack Finn collection.)

This c. 1910 image of Covina faces northeast toward the intersection of Citrus Street and Badillo Avenue. While the streetcars may be gone, Covina has proudly preserved many of its historic buildings and has an active and friendly historical society. On March 8, 1947, the Covina Line closed, and then by 1950, the right-of-way from Los Angeles to Baldwin Park was abandoned. (Historical photograph courtesy of the Covina Valley Historical Society.)

Traveling north on Garey Avenue in Pomona, just north of Pearl Street, only the two-story residential building has survived since this c. 1940 image was captured. A Foothill Transit bus heads north along the same line the Pacific Electric Railway once served. (Historical photograph by Harold Stewart; courtesy of the Craig Rasmussen collection.)

It was uncommon for a four-car train to be seen like it is here, heading north on Garey Avenue and crossing the Union Pacific and Southern Pacific tracks. The photographer made note of the date (September 27, 1936), the car numbers (1214, 1205, 1204 and 1215), as well as the time (3:25 p.m.). In the modern view, an underpass prevents automobile traffic from being backed up due to current-day freight traffic. (Historical photograph by Ralph Melching; courtesy of the PRS collection.)

This view looks north on Euclid Avenue at Holt Boulevard in Ontario around 1913, before car 177, shown in the earlier image, was renumbered to 817. Pullman built this style of car, which was commonly referred to as a "submarine" by the PE crews. This was because they were the first metal-bodied cars and also because the US Navy opened the first West Coast submarine base around the same time. (Historical photograph courtesy of the Jack Finn collection.)

EASTERN DISTRICT

Railroad Post Office cars (RPOs) were run by the Pacific Electric from 1905 through 1950. But on this line, they only ran from 1947 to 1950, as seen here with car 1407 next to the Rialto Station. Note the dash sign that reads, "U.S. Mail." The current image shows the station with little perceptible change. However, it is now a Mexican restaurant called Cuca's #4 Bar and Grill. (Historical photograph by Jack Whitmeyer; courtesy of the Donald Duke collection.)

68　Eastern District

The earlier photograph was originally shot on April 17, 1939. Seventy-two years to the day later, photographer Steve Crise went to Rialto Avenue to capture the modern image. The vintage picture shows boxmotor 1451 as it heads east, almost to its destination at San Bernardino, just having crossed the Union Pacific tracks. Today, Metrolink uses most of the same tracks from Los Angeles to San Bernardino. (Historical photograph by Charles D. Savage; courtesy of the Donald Duke collection.)

EASTERN DISTRICT

When the Atchison, Topeka & Santa Fe Railroad opened its San Bernardino station in 1918, it was the largest one west of the Mississippi; today, it serves Metrolink and Amtrak. Looking northeast, the modern image shows a local bus where PE car 105 once ran. Both of them service the Colton–San Bernardino Line area. For a brief time, there was an adjoining Harvey House, which closed in the 1950s. (Historical photograph courtesy of the Jack Finn collection.)

As a teen, Donald Duke traveled with his family to visit his Aunt Edna, and on the way home they photographed this Pacific Electric Railway steam locomotive (Southern Pacific no. 1817) making its way eastbound on Rialto Avenue at Giovanola Avenue on October 24, 1945. For every steam locomotive the PE used, an electric locomotive had to follow to trigger the signals and crossings. (Historical photograph courtesy of the Donald Duke collection.)

Arrowhead and Puritas Waters, both marketed throughout the Southern California area, shared their natural spring in the San Bernardino Mountains near the Arrowhead Springs Hotel. Electric locomotive 1591 is heading north up D Street at Third Street to fill empty tank cars with water for bottling sometime during the 1940s. Nothing remains of the old buildings downtown, and the Arrowhead Line was torn up in 1960. (Historical photograph by Jack Whitmeyer; courtesy of the Donald Duke collection.)

Business car 1299 pauses at the Pacific Electric/Southern Pacific Colton Station during this fan trip on August 5, 1951. The city's namesake is Civil War general David Colton, who was also the vice president of the Southern Pacific Railroad Company. The station survives, though boarded up today, and is near the intersection of 9th Street at Interstate 10. Car 1299 also survives today at Orange Empire Railway Museum (OERM). (Historical photograph by Andy "A.M." Payne; courtesy of the Jack Finn collection.)

EASTERN DISTRICT

Looking north on Market Street at Mission Inn Avenue, car 657 heads toward Arlington after leaving the Riverside Station in 1937. Legend has it that Hollywood types would travel here to preview movies, thereby avoiding negative reviews from film critics unwilling to travel that far. Riverside Station has survived in all its splendor, as has the neighboring Mission Inn. (Historical photograph Charles D. Savage; courtesy of the Donald Duke collection.)

CHAPTER 4

NORTHERN DISTRICT

In 1908, Charles Lawrence, official photographer for the Pacific Electric, took this iconic picture of car 401 stopped at the Sierra Madre Station near the corner of Baldwin Avenue and Sierra Madre Boulevard, just below the Mount Wilson Trail. Several stops in the Northern District included places nestled in the San Gabriel Mountains. (Historical photograph by Charles Lawrence; courtesy of the Mount Lowe Preservation Society, Inc.)

The Pacific Electric Railway building is the backdrop for this pair of images shot in downtown Los Angeles at Sixth and Main Streets. Car 1051 started out on the Pasadena Short Line, headed west on Sixth Street, turned right on Main Street, and headed north in this c. 1940s image. The PE building has recently completed a renovation to residential lofts. (Historical photograph courtesy of the Jack Finn collection.)

Car 1051 has made its way from the Pacific Electric Station at Sixth and Main Streets and exits the viaduct onto San Pedro Street, heading out to Pasadena via the Short Line around 1940. Looking southwest, the recent completion of the Rainbow Apartments has taken all of the history out of the modern-day image and blocks the view of the PE Lofts. (Historical photograph courtesy of the Jack Finn collection.)

NORTHERN DISTRICT

There was little fanfare on March 15, 1951, when car 1113 traveled along these tracks from the Aliso Street Viaduct. Most people didn't know these were the final days for the Monrovia-Glendora Line, as well as the end of the 1100-class car. In the modern scene at the Cesar Chavez Avenue Bridge and Interstate 10, it's no longer so easy to spot Los Angeles City Hall, dwarfed by skyscrapers. (Historical photograph by George C. White; courtesy of the Jack Finn collection.)

Looking northeast from Figueroa Street at Marmion Way in Highland Park, the old Pasadena and Los Angeles Railway car is flagged across the Los Angeles and Salt Lake tracks in 1906. It was not until the Great Merger of 1911 that this line was incorporated into the Pacific Electric Railway. Though not seen in this image, the Metro Gold Line currently runs from Los Angeles to Pasadena near this site. (Historical photograph attributed to Charles Lawrence; courtesy of the Donald Duke collection.)

A 1940s photographer took this shot of the four tracks looking northeast, just east of Oneonta Station and junction, where modern day Fair Oaks Avenue meets Huntington Drive. Boxmotor 1465, a former SP Interurban Electric Railway (IER) car from the bay area, heads inbound near the Marengo Apartments, which are still standing in South Pasadena. In this area, Huntington Drive straddles the cities of South Pasadena and Alhambra. (Historical photograph courtesy of the Jack Finn collection.)

A two-car train (cars 5075 and 5085) heads up Fair Oaks Avenue at Columbia Street, passing Raymond Hill in South Pasadena. Looking southeast, the historical waiting station from the former Raymond Hotel, listed in the National Register of Historic Places, has survived all these years, and is now a bus stop. The apartment building in the background and some of the palm trees have survived as well. (Historical photograph courtesy of the Jack Finn collection.)

Looking south on Fair Oaks Avenue toward Green Street, not much has changed with the historic Hotel Green since this photograph was taken in the 1940s. Car 1149 is heading north toward Colorado Boulevard, which is just another block away. A Metro bus still serves this line and can be seen where the trolley car was located in the earlier image. Modern-day Pasadena is still served by light rail with the Metro Gold Line. (Historical photograph courtesy of the Jack Finn collection)

Looking north at Lake and Mariposa Streets in Altadena, many of the historic buildings have remained intact. Car 460 is heading toward downtown Los Angeles via the Pasadena Short Line. This arched window car was one of the last built in the Los Angeles and Redondo shops. It was scrapped in 1940. (Historical photograph courtesy Michael Patris collection.)

Not many people remember the center of Huntington Drive in San Marino being home to multiple train stops and four rows of tracks. Car 1150 leads a two-car train from Pasadena to Los Angeles via Oak Knoll in 1945. Most of the buildings on the south side of the street remain today, but Market Basket supermarket has since been a video rental store and is currently a bank. (Historical photograph Donald Duke; courtesy of the Donald Duke collection.)

The snow of November 1949 was quite a rare occurrence, but tracks in the 900 block of Old Mill Road east of Oak Knoll Avenue have now become an urban legend. Looking north, homes were built on the former right-of-way, and the only clue to the spot's prior history is a raised area in the street where the ballasted tracks used to be. (Historical photograph Harold Stewart; courtesy of the Donald Duke collection.)

A young Donald Duke took out his new Graflex-D camera to shoot this c. 1948 image facing south on Oak Knoll Avenue near the old Huntington Hotel (now the Langham Huntington). In the historical image, the clock tower at Southwestern Military Academy in San Marino can be seen, just above the end of the 1100-class car. Part of the old right-of-way has become a water tank storage yard. (Historical photograph by Donald Duke; courtesy of the Donald Duke collection.)

The intersection of Oak Knoll Avenue and Canon Drive in Pasadena doesn't look the same as it once did, and few residents remember the PE cars going up and down the street until September 30, 1951. This line had been in operation since 1906 and was acquired as part of the Great Merger of 1911. Metro bus line 485 continues to travel this road and links Pasadena with Los Angeles. (Historical photograph courtesy of the Donald Duke collection.)

NORTHERN DISTRICT

Looking east from San Marino Avenue and Huntington Drive in San Marino, this area is just down the hill from the Huntington Library, former home of Pacific Electric Railway founder Henry Huntington. Car 1110 is heading inbound past the San Marino Times Building and near the current San Marino City Hall location. In the modern image, further east, the curved facade of San Marino Pharmacy still stands at Ridgeway Road and Huntington Drive. (Historical photograph courtesy of the Jack Finn collection.)

Originally, a horse car line along Myrtle Avenue serviced Monrovia. It later became electrified, offering regular service in 1903. This 1100-class car is in front of the Monrovia Station, but the station is out of sight looking north. The car is heading west on Olive Avenue, where it will continue on to San Marino and then downtown Los Angeles. Service was discontinued on this line on September 30, 1951. (Historical photograph courtesy of the Jack Finn collection.)

In front of what once was the Bradbury Estate, car 1105 heads west through the trench at Duarte and toward downtown Los Angeles. The Pacific Electric built this bridge in 1908 following an extension of its line. Currently, this concrete bridge is only open to foot traffic, having closed to automobiles about 1960. Originally, according to a plaque, the bridge was 90 feet long, 22 feet wide, and 23 feet above the roadbed. (Historical photograph courtesy of the Jack Finn collection.)

The Pacific Electric bridged the San Gabriel River in 1907, appropriately naming its new structure Puente Largo, Spanish for "long bridge." 8,000 cubic feet of concrete spanned 1,019 feet for this double-track, standard-gauge bridge. The metal replacement section in the foreground was constructed due to extreme flooding when three piers were lost in 1938. In the modern image, local plein air landscape artist Lee Edwards frequents the bridge area for artistic inspiration. (Historical photograph courtesy of the Jack Finn collection.)

Car 1122 pauses near the corner of Ninth Street and Azusa Avenue near the old Azusa Passenger and Freight Depot in this c. 1940s photograph. The modern image shows how the area has evolved but doesn't reveal how the Metro Gold Line Extension will open in the near future to once again serve this community with light rail transportation. (Historical photograph courtesy of the Jack Finn collection.)

Looking west on Main Street, the "Alhambra" sign denotes the city's eastern limit. The Alhambra Wash passes under this spot, separating it from the city of San Gabriel. This image of car 1002 was captured on March 5, 1941, just months before the line closed on November 29, 1941. The small Spanish-style building on the north side of the street remains, just above the banks of the now-cemented wash. (Historical photograph by Wilbur "Will" C. Whittaker; courtesy of Jack Finn collection.)

The San Gabriel Mission was built in 1771, and tourists have enjoyed it ever since. Tilton Trolley Trips made frequent stops in front of it as part of its "100 miles for 100 cents" tour. Car 04 pauses just long enough for a photograph, and then continues on its "From the Sea to the Orange Groves" excursion. Cars beginning with a zero were for touring, not for regular service. (Historical photograph courtesy of the Jack Finn collection.)

Temple City's Chamber of Commerce opened for business in March 1924, just in time to convince the Pacific Electric to extend the Alhambra-San Gabriel Line to their town. The extension ran east along Las Tunas Drive to Kauffman Avenue, where it looped back west. The station is long gone, and city hall now occupies that land. This photograph of car 1010 was taken in the 1940s, shortly before the line closed in November 1941. (Historical photograph courtesy of the Jack Finn collection.)

NORTHERN DISTRICT

www.arcadiapublishing.com

Discover books about the town where you grew up, the cities where your friends and families live, the town where your parents met, or even that retirement spot you've been dreaming about. Our Web site provides history lovers with exclusive deals, advanced notification about new titles, e-mail alerts of author events, and much more.

Arcadia Publishing, the leading local history publisher in the United States, is committed to making history accessible and meaningful through publishing books that celebrate and preserve the heritage of America's people and places. Consistent with our mission to preserve history on a local level, this book was printed in South Carolina on American-made paper and manufactured entirely in the United States.

This book carries the accredited Forest Stewardship Council (FSC) label and is printed on 100 percent FSC-certified paper. Products carrying the FSC label are independently certified to assure consumers that they come from forests that are managed to meet the social, economic, and ecological needs of present and future generations.

Cert no. SW-COC-001530
www.fsc.org
© 1996 Forest Stewardship Council

Find Your Place in History.